Dedicated To:

This Wonderful

Day:

Love

With love From:

You are special
to me,

you are my
heart,

You are my
everything.

Blooming like
a flower in
Spring

You have
become my
entire heart,

My true
everything.

Every day I
celebrate you;

I sing and dance

and when we

are apart

I carry you right here inside my heart.

What I Love About You

What I love most about you:

You hold a special place in my heart:

One very special thing about you is:

What I know about you:

Your dear and wonderful qualities are:

You are a rare gem because:

Amazingly, you are the only person who:

Precious and priceless, you are:

One very unique quality about you is:

What I admire most about you:

You are special to me and the world:

One wonderful trait you have is:

You are like no one else:

A shining star you are:

One amazing thing about you is:

I love you:

You are my heart:

You are special:

I love you:

You are my heart:

You are special:

I ♥
YOU

Enjoy the other titles by Julian Vincent:

I Love You

Happy, Happy, Happy Birthday

Happy, Happy, Happy Birthday Coupons

You Are Special, You Are My Heart

Fluffy, Snuggly, Kind, It's Christmas Time!

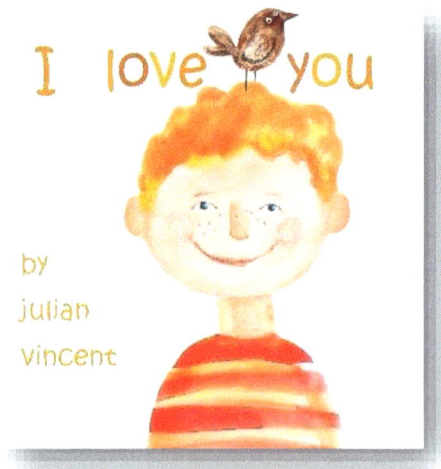

I love you

by
julian
vincent

Love

To my sweetie, this is for you.   To loma, this is for you.   To gosling, this is for you.

Published by TeK. Published in the USA

www.ingramcontent.com/pod-product-compliance
Lightning Source LLC
Chambersburg PA
CBHW061354090426
42739CB00002B/29